D1400443

LONDON PUBLIC LIBRARY

Good
DOG!

NICOLA JANE SWINNEY

FIREFLY BOOKS

A FIREFLY BOOK

Published by Firefly Books Ltd., 2019
Text © Nicola Jane Swinney
Copyright © Marshall Editions 2016

All rights reserved. No part of this publication may be reproduced, stored in a retrieval system, or transmitted in any form or by any means, electronic, mechanical, photocopying, recording or otherwise, without the prior written permission of the Publisher.

First printing

Library of Congress Control Number: 2019938802

Library and Archives Canada Cataloguing in Publication
Title: Good dog! / Nicola Jane Swinney.
Names: Swinney, Nicola Jane, author.
Description: Includes index.
Identifiers: Canadiana 20190098570 | ISBN 9780228102137 (softcover)
Subjects: LCSH: Dogs—Juvenile literature. | LCSH: Dog breeds—Juvenile literature.
Classification: LCC SF426.5 .S95 2019 | DDC j636.7—dc23

Published in Canada by
Firefly Books Ltd.
50 Staples Avenue, Unit 1
Richmond Hill, Ontario
L4B 0A7

Published in the United States by
Firefly Books (U.S.) Inc.
P.O. Box 1338, Ellicott Station
Buffalo, New York
14205

Printed in China

Photographic Acknowledgments

With the exception of the following, all images are courtesy of Bob Langrish Images.

Front cover: Superstock/Juniors

bg = background, t = top, b = bottom, r = right,
l = left, m = middle.

Alamy: 5tr Thorsten Eckert; 5mr Simon Hadley. Dreamstime: Anke Van Wyk 29r, 84-85bg; Onetouchspark 45mr; Kseniya Ragozina 61br; Dmitrijs Gerciks 65br; Eros Erika 68-69bg; Sasha Skvortsova 70bg; Wei Wang 71tr; Sergey Bogdanov 71br; Roughcollie 73br; AnnaUtekhina 86-87bg; Sunheyy 91tr; Rita Soti 93mr; Vkarlov 93br; Oleg Banniko 94-95bg. Getty Images: 4-5bg Brand X Pictures. Shutterstock: Ksenia Raykova 2-3, 59r; 4bl Margo Harrison; Tina Rencelj 6-7; Martin Maun 10-11bg, WilleeCole Photography 12-13bg; Rita Kochmarjova 13tr, 64bl; Lindsay Helms 13br; Paul Wishart 14bg; anetapics 15br; Zuzule 16bl, 91br; Margarita Zhuravleva 17tr; Natalia V Guseva 18-19bg; SJ Allen 19br; Dunhill 28-29bg; otsphoto 30b, 45tr, 59br; Labrador Photo Video 30-31bg; Daz Stock 31tr; Capture Light 32-33bg, 35tr, 88-89bg; godrick 34-35bg; Javier Brosch 35mr; Vladimir Nenezic 38b; Tad Denson 38 -39bg, 50-51bg; pixshots 39tr; Margojh 39b; Dennis Jacobsen 40-41bg; gillmar 41mr; Jiri Vaclavek 41br; Degtyaryov Andrey 43br; YamabikaY 44bl; Best dog photo 56-57bg; grahamspics 58bl; Julianne Caust 59tr; Marcel Jancovic 60br, 60-61bg, 61tr; Natalia Rezanova 62br; Abramova Kseniya 62-63bg; Stanimir G.Stoev 63tr; Ewais 63mr; Vivienstock 63br; MF Photo 66bg; Liliya Kulianionak 67mr, 80bg, 82-83bg; YAN WEN 71mr; Annette Kurka 72bl; Goldika 75tr; cynoclub 80bl; PolinaBright 87tr; Grisha Bruev 87mr; Mitrofanov Alexander 87br; Everita Pane 88bl, 89mr; Anna Goroshnikova 89tr; mariait 89br; Olga_i 90-91bg; Agris Krusts 91mr; Kozub Vasyl 92bl; Waldemar Dabrowski 94bl; Ekaterina Brusnika 96bg; Sbolotova gfl; Alexandra Baklamina gfbr; Lenkadan 58bg; AlohaHawaii 58tr; Anneka 59l; Reddogs 59tr.

CONTENTS

^A DOG BY OUR SIDE

It is said that the dog is the only creature on Earth that will love you more than it loves itself. Anyone who has ever owned a dog would say that this is true. The look of absolute joy on your dog's face when you return from an epic journey—or even just from going to the store to buy milk—tells you everything you need to know.

CONSTANT COMPANIONS

The dog is our most constant companion, and we love to show it off on the show bench. But many dogs have a far more important role to play. Whether for warmth or for work, for guarding or for herding, for thousands of years, dogs have served us well. Where would we be today without guide dogs for the blind and the deaf, the search and rescue dogs that save lives, or the sniffer dogs that prevent terrible crimes? Our lives would truly be much emptier without our canine companions.

LOVED AND CHERISHED

Through their hard work and devotion, it is the dog's love for us, rather than the other way round, that has defined our relationship with this most selfless of creatures. It is up to us to return the favor, to take good care of them and to make sure they know how much we love them back.

5

Popular
Pets

It is thought that humans first tamed the gray wolf around 33,000 years ago, and since then the dog—whose Latin name is *Canis lupus familiaris*—has been our constant companion. Here are some of the favorite breeds to keep as pets.

THE GERMAN SHEPHERD

An American soldier, Corporal Lee Duncan, found a tiny puppy in France during World War I. At the end of the war Duncan took him home to Los Angeles. That puppy became Rin Tin Tin, a television and movie star who received more than 10,000 fan letters a week at the height of his fame. Rin Tin Tin was a German Shepherd, and his legend is part of the reason that the German Shepherd is so popular in America today.

THE SHEEPHERDING DOG

The German Shepherd is a fairly new breed, dating back to 1899. Max von Stephanitz, a captain in the German cavalry, decided to create a breed that would serve as a sheepherding dog. He knew that German farmers relied on their dogs to protect their flocks of sheep as well as herding them. Although these farmers would travel miles to mate their female dog with a suitable male, no one had tried to breed a distinct type.

THE NEW BREED

Von Stephanitz studied the breeding techniques of the British, who were renowned for their herding dogs. Meanwhile, he traveled widely to dog shows searching for what he considered the ideal sheepherder, and one day found a dog called Hektor Linksrhein. He bought the dog, renamed it Horand von Grafeth, and formed a society, the Society for German Shepherd Dogs, in which he would register Horand's offspring. The German Shepherd dog was born.

FACT FILE

COLOR: shades of sandy brown and black, all black, all white

SIZE (MALE ADULT): 60 pounds (27 kilograms)

HEIGHT AT SHOULDER: 24 inches (61 centimeters)

LIFESPAN: about 14 years

CHARACTER: intelligent, loyal, devoted

A WAR HERO

As farming became increasingly mechanized, the need for sheepherding dogs declined. Von Stephanitz approached the German government and persuaded it to use his breed in the police and military. In World War I alone, about 48,000 German Shepherd dogs were enlisted into the German army. Some were captured by American soldiers and later taken home to the United States. Devoted and faithful, a German Shepherd is a courageous and intelligent dog that makes a wonderful companion, but it does tend to be loyal to just one person.

9

THE LABRADOR RETRIEVER

If the phrase "man's best friend" were to describe any specific breed, it would probably be the Labrador Retriever. Gentle and friendly, loyal and trusting, the breed came from the island of Newfoundland, off the northeastern coast of Canada. It was bred to help the local fishermen by hauling nets, fetching ropes, and retrieving fish.

ALMOST LOST

Originally known as the "St. John's dog," after the island's capital city, the Labrador Retriever disappeared from Newfoundland because the government only allowed families to keep one dog. Female dogs were highly taxed, so many bitch puppies were culled. By the 1880s, despite its usefulness as a working dog and as a calm companion, the breed was almost extinct.

AMERICA'S NUMBER ONE

Today, the Labrador Retriever is the most popular breed with the American Kennel Club and is in demand both as a family pet and as a working dog. Labrador Retrievers are energetic dogs who need a lot of exercise, but they are good-natured, and most are patient with children. The breed has also found favor in England.

THE OTTER TAIL

One distinctive feature of the Labrador Retriever is its tail, which is very thick toward the base, tapering to the tip. It is thickly coated all over with short, dense hair, which gives it a rounded appearance. This is described as an "otter" tail and is a highly desirable trait in the breed.

FACT FILE

COLOR: yellow, black, chocolate, red

SIZE (MALE ADULT): 60 pounds (27 kilograms)

HEIGHT AT SHOULDER: 24 inches (61 centimeters)

LIFESPAN: about 10 years

CHARACTER: gentle, biddable, friendly, calm

THE BULLDOG

First identified in 1603, the Bulldog is one of Great Britain's oldest native breeds. There are even earlier mentions of dogs of a similar type that were known as "bandogs," a word that now refers to a kind of fighting dog. The Bulldog was originally used for bullbaiting, a sport that was popular in the 1700s.

BULLBAITING

The practice of bullbaiting involved tying up a bull and encouraging dogs to bite and attack it. Although today we find it cruel, bullbaiting was more than just entertainment—it was thought to help tenderize the meat. There was even a law that stated that "no butcher shall kill any bull two years old [and] upward, unless he first be brought to the ring and sufficiently baited." Bullbaiting was outlawed in 1835, but owners continued to use their bulldogs to fight other dogs for entertainment.

BRITISH MASCOT

With its endearingly "ugly" face and stocky foursquare stance, the Bulldog is a popular symbol of Great Britain. It sums up the determined British spirit and its stubborn heart. The breed first entered the show benches in 1860, where it became a hit.

FACT FILE

COLOR: solid color, smut, brindle, red, fawn, pied

SIZE (MALE ADULT): 55 pounds (25 kilograms)

HEIGHT AT SHOULDER: 15 inches (38 centimeters)

LIFESPAN: about 10 years

CHARACTER: bold, loyal, brave

LOYAL FAMILY DOG

The Bulldog does have a stubborn streak, but it is also loving and brave. It is good-tempered with children and has a playful nature, so it will happily join in with family games. The modern dogs are shorter-faced than their fighting ancestors, and more squat in the body.

THE BEAGLE

The name "Beagle" may have come from the French term *be'geule*, meaning "gape throat," referring to the dog's baying voice. Or it could be a reference to the dog's size, which could come from the French word *beigh*, the Old English *begele*, or the Celtic word *beag*, all of which mean "small."

A MERRY LITTLE DOG

Beagles have been bred since the 1500s to hunt for small prey, accompanied by men on foot. The dogs tracked rabbits, hare, pheasant, quail, and other animals. Beagles are still sometimes used as hunting dogs, and a few colleges and schools in England still have a Beagle pack. But unlike many other hound types, Beagles make wonderful pets because of their happy-go-lucky nature.

FACT FILE

COLOR: black, tan and white, red and white

SIZE (MALE ADULT):
30 pounds (13.6 kilograms)

HEIGHT AT SHOULDER:
15 inches (38 centimeters)

LIFESPAN: about 15 years

CHARACTER: gentle, playful, sweet-tempered

POCKET ROCKETS

During the reigns of King Henry VIII and Queen Elizabeth I in England, tiny wirehaired Beagles were common. Some of them were small enough to be carried in the pocket of a hunting jacket. Adult Beagles now stand up to 15 inches (38 centimeters) at the shoulder, but smaller versions—called "pocket Beagles"—do sometimes still occur.

A WORKING ASSET

Because of its extremely strong sense of smell, the Beagle is in demand as a sniffer dog. Since 1984, the U.S. Department of Agriculture has used Beagles to sniff out food being illegally brought into the country. Beagles have also been used to detect drugs and explosives.

THE YORKSHIRE TERRIER

Known as "the little dog with the big personality," the Yorkie—to use its affectionate nickname—lives up to its billing. It is the most popular toy dog breed in the United States and, because of its size, is very well suited to apartment living.

LOOKING FOR ADVENTURE

With its long, silky, steel-blue coat—and sometimes sporting a perky topknot—the Yorkie is an attractive little creature, but it doesn't know it's a small dog! It thinks it's much bigger than it is, and can sometimes bite off more than it can chew. But it is affectionate and playful, so it makes a loving pet.

RATTING DOGS

The Yorkshire Terrier is thought to have been the result of cross-breeding between different types of Terriers from Scotland, which were brought to England during the Industrial Revolution of the late 18th and early 19th centuries. They were probably kept to catch rats in factories.

THE FATHER OF THE YORKIE

A dog that was called a "broken-haired Scotch Terrier" appeared at a show in 1861. It may have been a Yorkie. Huddersfield Ben, who was born in 1865, is considered the "father" of the modern breed. The breed was first referred to as the Yorkshire Terrier in 1870, and they were first recorded in the United States in 1872.

FACT FILE

COLOR: steel-blue and tan

SIZE (MALE ADULT):
6 pounds (2.7 kilograms)

HEIGHT AT SHOULDER:
9 inches (23 centimeters)

LIFESPAN: about 15 years

CHARACTER: lively, loving, brave

THE POODLE

When you see an elegant Poodle on the show bench, you might think that it never gets those perfect paws dirty. But the Poodle was bred to be a duck dog, jumping into water to retrieve birds shot by hunters. Its name comes from the German word *pudel*, which means to splash in water.

DUCKS AND TRUFFLES

Although it came from the marshes of Germany, the Poodle's country of origin is listed as France, where it arrived with German soldiers centuries ago. The French call it the *caniche*, which comes from *chien canard*, meaning "duck dog." It was also used to sniff out truffles underground.

THREE SIZES

There are three sizes of Poodle: Standard, Miniature, and Toy. However, they are all considered to be the same breed. The Standard Poodle—similar in size to a Siberian Husky—is believed to be the original, with the smaller sizes bred in later. All are intelligent and eager to learn.

FACT FILE

COLOR: blue, gray, silver, brown, café au lait, cream, apricot, red, black, white

SIZE (MALE ADULT):
70 pounds (32 kilograms)

HEIGHT AT SHOULDER:
22 inches (56 centimeters)

LIFESPAN: about 15 years

CHARACTER: playful, happy, home-loving

A PRACTICAL CLIP

The Poodles that you see on a show bench have their coats clipped in a distinctive way, but the traditional Poodle clip is not just for appearance. Taking the thick, curling coat off its body allows a dog to swim more freely, while the hair left on its joints and vital organs protect it in cold water.

THE BOXER

The Boxer comes from Germany, where its name, *Bullenbeisser*, means "bull-biter." In its home country, it was one of the first breeds selected for training to do police work. It is a large, muscular dog that looks imposing, although underneath it has a charming nature.

GUARD DOGS

Early Boxers were bred by wealthy landowners as hunting dogs to pursue boar and bears. Many of the large estates that bred them were broken up during and after the Napoleonic Wars of the early 1800s. The larger *Bullenbeisser* fell out of favor, but the smaller version was much in demand as a family pet and guard dog.

ENGLISH INFLUENCE

Paintings before 1830 show Boxer-type dogs colored fawn or brindle, with "black masks" on their faces, and no white markings at all. It is thought that English dogs taken to Germany after that time—including the Bulldog—introduced the white color. This is still seen in the breed, but large amounts of white are frowned on by judges.

FACT FILE

COLOR: fawn or brindle, with white

SIZE (MALE ADULT):
70 pounds (32 kilograms)

HEIGHT AT SHOULDER:
25 inches (64 centimeters)

LIFESPAN: about 12 years

CHARACTER: alert, fearless, friendly

PUPPY-LIKE CHARM

The boxer is sometimes called "the Peter Pan of the dog world," because it does not fully mature until it is about three years old, giving it one of the longest puppyhoods of all dog breeds. The boxer is naturally playful and can be a little boisterous, but does not usually have an aggressive nature.

Hounds
and
Hunting Dogs

It is likely that humans first tamed wild dogs to help with hunting, rather than for companionship. Today, some people still use hunting dogs to track deer, foxes, coyotes, rabbits, and other prey. The partnership between hunter and hound is known as the "golden thread."

THE GREYHOUND

The modern Greyhound is an elegant, instantly recognizable breed. Drawings of dogs that look very much like them have been found in Egyptian tombs dating back to 4000 B.C. They are believed to have originated in North Africa and the Middle East. The Greyhound is the only breed mentioned by name in the King James Bible.

A KING'S LAW

The first known mention of the breed in Europe dates back to the Dark Ages (476 A.D. to 800 A.D.). Before long, Greyhounds were so highly thought of for their hunting ability that by law, only noblemen were allowed to own them. Anyone who lived within 10 miles (16 kilometers) of the king's hunting forests was forbidden to own a greyhound.

THE SPORT OF COURSING

Using a dog to chase prey, usually a hare, was called coursing. It was a fashionable sport in England, and the speedy Greyhound was supremely suited to it. British colonists brought the dogs to the Americas, where coursing and racing both became popular. The first official coursing race in the United States took place in 1886 in Kansas.

BUILT FOR SPEED

Greyhounds are best known as racing dogs. They are tall and slender, built for speed, and they race by instinct. But for all their speed, they are gentle, loving creatures that are just as happy to lounge around at home. They are known as the "40-mile-per-hour couch potato!"

FACT FILE

COLOR: most solid colors, and parti-color

SIZE (MALE ADULT):
85 pounds (39 kilograms)

HEIGHT AT SHOULDER:
29 inches (74 centimeters)

LIFESPAN: about 12 years

CHARACTER: loving, gentle, calm

THE BASSET HOUND

Dignified and wise-looking, the Basset Hound comes from France, where its name means "short-legged" or "low-set." Both the Basset Hound and its long-legged cousin, the Bloodhound, are thought to be descendants of the famous Saint Hubert's Hounds.

SAINT HUBERT'S HOUNDS

Saint Hubert, the patron saint of hunters, was born in France in 656 A.D. "Saint Hubert's Hound" is now used as another name for one of its descendants, the Bloodhound. The Basset Hound is likely just a naturally short-legged version of the Bloodhound.

ENGAGING PERSONALITY

Unlike many other hunting hounds, the Basset Hound makes a lovely pet. It has an engaging personality and just loves people, even though its deep, baying bark might suggest otherwise!

WET AND WRINKLY

The Basset Hound has an endearingly wrinkled face but does tend to drool. It also slobbers when it drinks, so it is not the best choice of pet for a neat freak.

SCENTING ABILITY

A Basset Hound is a short dog with a long body, large head, soulful dark eyes, long ears, and a superb sense of smell. The Basset Hound is able to hunt through heavy vegetation and holds its nose close to the ground. It stands barely 15 inches (38 centimeters) at the shoulder but can weigh up to 70 pounds (32 kilograms), so it is a big dog on short legs.

FACT FILE

COLOR: black, tan and white, red and white, lemon and white, gray

SIZE (MALE ADULT):
70 pounds (32 kilograms)

HEIGHT AT SHOULDER:
15 inches (38 centimeters)

LIFESPAN: about 12 years

CHARACTER: friendly, gentle, intelligent

THE RHODESIAN RIDGEBACK

This handsome breed gets the first part of its name from its home in Rhodesia, the African country that is now known as Zimbabwe. A line of coarse hair that sticks up along its spine gives it the second part of its name. The breed's original purpose was to track large game animals, including lions, during big-game hunting trips.

THREE BREEDS

The distinctive ridge of fur is only seen in two other breeds, both of which come from southeast Asia: the Mah Thai Lang Ahn and the Phu Quoc Ridgeback. It is likely that the three breeds are related, though it's unclear whether the Rhodesian Ridgeback traveled east or the eastern ones were brought to Africa.

BREEDING A HUNTER

In Africa, the half-wild native dogs kept by the Khoikhoi people were crossed with Great Danes, Mastiffs, and Hounds to make the modern Ridgeback. Breeders noted that dogs with the ridge of hair made the best hunters. A Rhodesian hunter called Cornelius von Rooyen began a breeding program, and the breed standard was set in 1922.

POWERFUL AND INTELLIGENT

Ridgebacks are powerfully built dogs and, because they are intelligent, they can be trained for other jobs besides hunting. Ridgebacks are courageous, so they make excellent guard dogs. However, they do have a stubborn streak and can be destructive if they get bored.

FACT FILE

COLOR: buff, light gold, red-gold

SIZE (MALE ADULT):
85 pounds (39 kilograms)

HEIGHT AT SHOULDER:
27 inches (69 centimeters)

LIFESPAN: about 12 years

CHARACTER: intelligent, loyal, stubborn

THE COCKER SPANIEL

The "Lady" in the much-loved Disney movie *Lady and the Tramp* is a Cocker Spaniel, and she is portrayed as being beautiful and charming, which is exactly what the breed is like. The Cocker Spaniel is the smallest of the American Kennel Club sporting breeds and makes a delightful companion.

A SPANISH DOG

The Cocker Spaniel was originally a working gundog. It gets its name because it was used to flush woodcock, a popular game bird, out of the underbrush. The name "spaniel" means "Spanish dog," and it is thought all spaniels originally came from Spain. The Cocker Spaniel was first recognized as a separate breed in 1892.

INTO THE AMERICAS

American dog fanciers started importing English Cocker Spaniels to the United States in the late 1870s. As the breed became popular, two different types appeared: the traditional English one and a smaller, flashier version, ideal for the show bench.

EAGER TO PLEASE

Alert and bright, it is no surprise that the Cocker Spaniel is a popular pet. Its origin as a working dog means that it will happily retrieve things around the house—such as a toy or a slipper—and will then wag its tail, waiting for praise. It is an affectionate little dog, too, trying to please its owner.

FACT FILE

COLOR: solid colors, parti or bicolors, roans

SIZE (MALE ADULT): 32 pounds (15 kilograms)

HEIGHT AT SHOULDER: 16 inches (41 centimeters)

LIFESPAN: about 15 years

CHARACTER: happy, loyal, lively

THE DACHSHUND

The writer H. L. Mencken once said that the adorable "wiener dog" is "half a dog high and a dog and a half long." But despite its unusual appearance, the Dachshund was bred for a purpose—to hunt animals such as badgers. *Dachs* is German for "badger."

POPULAR DOG

The Dachshund is the size of a terrier but has the tracking ability of a hound, making it perfect for tracking badgers. Before World War I, it was one of the top ten most popular dog breeds in the United States, but after the war, anti-German feeling meant that it fell out of favor. People started to call it the "badger dog" to avoid associating it with Germany.

SIZE MATTERS

The Dachshund comes in three coat types: smooth-haired, wire-haired, and long-haired. In the United States, there are two sizes, standard and miniature, while in Germany the sizes are distinguished not by weight but by chest measurement, which shows what size of hole the dog could enter when chasing prey.

FACT FILE

COLOR: black and tan, red, chocolate, tan

SIZE (MALE ADULT): 30 pounds (14 kilograms)

HEIGHT AT SHOULDER: 9 inches (23 centimeters)

LIFESPAN: about 15 years

CHARACTER: alert, curious, friendly

AN ENERGETIC PET

Despite its small size, the Dachshund is not likely to tire from exercise—you're more likely to want to go home after a walk than an energetic little Dachshund! But it is always happy to be in your company and is a loyal family pet.

THE JACK RUSSELL

In 1819, a hunting clergyman named the Reverend John "Jack" Russell bought a terrier called Trump. Trump was white with markings on its head and tail, and he sired a legacy of sporting terriers. This little dog is considered the founder of the Jack Russell breed.

GOING TO GROUND

The Jack Russell was bred to dig into the ground and was often used alongside packs of fox-hunting dogs. The hunter could carry the dog in a pannier on his saddle, but the terrier also needed stamina to keep up with the hounds if necessary. If a fox escaped into a hole, the terrier would be sent to chase after him.

TWO RUSSELL BREEDS

The Jack Russell was recognized by the British Kennel Club in 2015, while the American Kennel Club recognizes a breed called the Parson Russell. The Parson Russell was once considered a longer-legged version of the Jack Russell, but is now thought of as a separate breed.

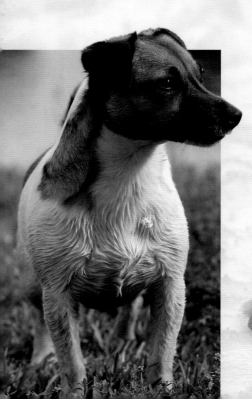

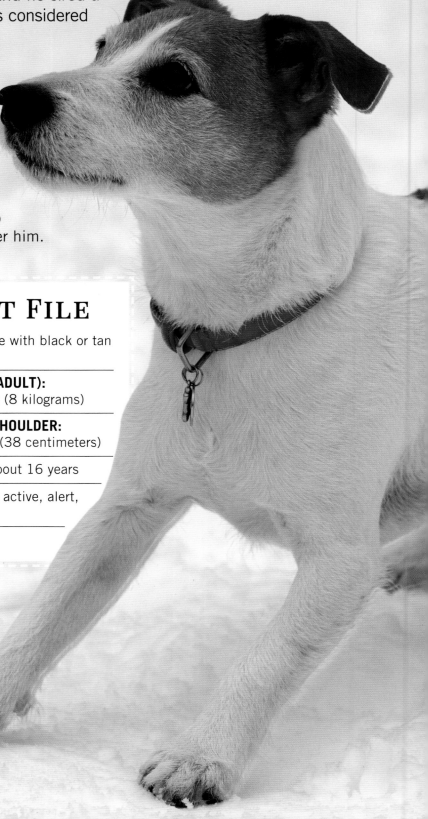

FACT FILE

COLOR: white with black or tan markings

SIZE (MALE ADULT): 18 pounds (8 kilograms)

HEIGHT AT SHOULDER: 15 inches (38 centimeters)

LIFESPAN: about 16 years

CHARACTER: active, alert, playful

WHO'S THE BOSS?

The Jack Russell is generally a cheerful, devoted dog that loves to be part of the family. It does, however, have a stubborn streak and needs a firm hand in training. A Jack Russell with the right temperament can be a wonderful pet, but some will always want to be the boss, causing problems with other pets or children.

Pocket–Sized
Companions

While some people love the bigger dog breeds, there is something delightful about the miniatures. These cute little creatures can sometimes fit in a purse, but they have big personalities to contrast with their tiny size.

THE BICHON FRISE

The ancestors of this adorable little dog were first discovered by sailors in the Canary Islands in the 14th century. For a while it was called the "Tenerife Dog" after one of the islands. Many people believe that the Bichon Frise is related to the Barbet, a water dog, which was sometimes called the *Barbichon*.

ROYAL FAVORITE

In the 16th century, King Henry III of France owned Bichons Frises and was so fond of them that he carried them everywhere with him in a special basket hung from his neck. The breed was also popular with Spanish royalty, and featured in several paintings by the renowned Spanish artist Francisco de Goya.

BORN PERFORMER

The Bichon Frise remained popular with royalty until the late 1800s. After that, the breed became popular for doing tricks with street performers and circuses. Because the breed is highly intelligent, it was also trained as a guide dog to help lead the blind.

WONDERFUL PET

The Bichon Frise's double-layered coat makes it look like a walking powder puff. However, it also means that it needs a lot of grooming. The longer outer hairs can get trapped in the soft, dense undercoat, so it needs brushing regularly to keep it from getting matted. Coat maintenance aside, this charming little dog makes a wonderful pet—it loves people!

FACT FILE

COLOR: white

SIZE (MALE ADULT):
12 pounds (5 kilograms)

HEIGHT AT SHOULDER:
11 inches (28 centimeters)

LIFESPAN: about 15 years

CHARACTER: cheerful, intelligent, devoted

THE CHIHUAHUA

It might be the world's smallest dog breed, but it has one of the biggest personalities! The enchanting Chihuahua was found in the Mexican state from which it takes its name, but its exact origins are not clear. It is possible that it is descended from small dogs called *techichi.* Carvings of these dogs from the 9th century show the similarities between the two breeds.

MAGICAL POWERS

The *techichi* carvings were made by the Toltec, a civilization that lived in Central America. The Aztecs eventually conquered the Toltec, and they adopted their little dogs. The *techichi* lived in Aztec temples and were used in rituals. The Aztecs believed the dogs had magical powers, including the ability to see into the future.

FACT FILE

COLOR: all colors

SIZE (MALE ADULT):
6 pounds (3 kilograms)

HEIGHT AT SHOULDER:
9 inches (23 centimeters)

LIFESPAN: about 18 years

CHARACTER: alert, loving, loyal

AMERICAN HIT

The first Chihuahuas appeared in the United States in the 1890s, when visitors to Mexico brought the tiny dogs back with them. A Chihuahua named Midget was the first to be registered with the American Kennel Club, in 1904. Long-haired versions started to crop up, probably the result of crosses with Papillons or Pomeranians.

LOTS OF EXERCISE

While the Chihuahua makes a loyal and devoted pet, it is not without its issues—it can be very destructive, especially if it is left alone. The breed is trainable, and its tiny size makes it suited to apartment living, but you may be surprised by the amount of exercise this little dog needs!

THE PAPILLON

The Papillon was a popular subject for European painters from the 16th to 18th centuries, who often depicted the dogs sitting on the laps of their adoring mistresses. The breed originally had dropped ears and was called the *Epagneul Nain* or "dwarf spaniel."

BUTTERFLY DOG

It is the unique shape of the ears that gives this prettiest of dogs its name. In the 17th century court of Louis XIV of France, a small spaniel with upright ears was developed named *Papillon*, which is French for "butterfly." The dog's erect, fringed ears are said to resemble butterfly wings. It was also sometimes called the "squirrel dog," because of its long, plumed tail.

CONTINENTAL SPANIEL

Both varieties, either with upright ears or with dropped ears, were for a time called continental toy spaniels. The version with the erect ears was known as Papillon, while the one with dropped ears was called *Phalene*, which means "moth." The two types can sometimes be born in the same litter of puppies, but *Phalenes* are now rare.

FACT FILE

COLOR: white with colored patches

SIZE (MALE ADULT):
9 pounds (4 kilograms)

HEIGHT AT SHOULDER:
11 inches (28 centimeters)

LIFESPAN: about 16 years

CHARACTER: willing, intelligent, affectionate

A PEOPLE DOG

Despite its delicate appearance, the Papillon is not merely a lapdog. It is lively and curious, always looking for mischief. It is a people-loving dog, good with children and other pets, but seeks lots of attention. Despite its long coat, it does not need regular grooming.

THE POMERANIAN

The original Pomeranians—named after a region on the Baltic Sea that lies between Germany and Poland—were much bigger than the modern breed, weighing up to 30 pounds (14 kilograms). It is the smallest member of the spitz family of dogs, which includes the sled dogs of Iceland and Lapland.

FAMOUS FANS

The Pomeranian has had many well-known admirers. Michelangelo is said to have painted the Sistine Chapel with his dog curled up nearby on a satin pillow. Chopin composed the "Minute Waltz"—originally called the "Little Dog Waltz"—after watching a Pomeranian chasing its tail. Queen Victoria of England owned dozens of the little dogs. As she lay dying, her favorite Pomeranian, Turi, was brought to her bedside.

GROOMING

A Pomeranian's soft, fluffy fur needs lots of care with special dog shampoos and conditioners. It must not be brushed when dry, and the routine should be: comb, brush, comb.

FACT FILE

COLOR: all colors (red and gold most common)

SIZE (MALE ADULT):
7 pounds (3 kilograms)

HEIGHT AT SHOULDER:
12 inches (30 centimeters)

LIFESPAN: about 16 years

CHARACTER: bold, curious, social

EASILY TRAINED

There is nothing the Pomeranian loves more than meeting new people! It is a bold, outgoing little dog whose curious nature makes it enthusiastic about getting involved in everything. It makes a good family pet and will happily live in an apartment. It is intelligent and easy to train—Pomeranians also perform in dog agility competitions.

THE PUG

Snub-nosed dogs have always been popular in China, where the Pug is thought to come from. Prized by the emperors of China, these dogs lived in luxurious homes and were sometimes even guarded by soldiers. Later, they were kept as pets in monasteries.

MIGHTY ANCESTORS

There were three types of snub-nosed dogs in China: the lion dog, the Pekingese, and the Lo-Sze. Similar dogs were also found in Tibet and Japan, and the mighty Tibetan Mastiff may be related to the tiny Pug. The Pug's name comes from the Latin word meaning "fist."

A LIFE-SAVER

Traders brought the Pug to Europe, and a Pug called Hermingny was credited with saving the life of William, Prince of Orange. It barked at approaching Spanish troops, alerting him to their presence. As a result of its heroism, it became the official dog of the House of Orange in Holland. Later, the prince went to England as King William III, and took his Pugs with him.

FACT FILE

COLOR: all solid colors

SIZE (MALE ADULT):
20 pounds (9 kilograms)

HEIGHT AT SHOULDER:
13 inches (33 centimeters)

LIFESPAN: about 15 years

CHARACTER: playful, loving, sociable

A DOG FOR LIFE

The Pug is known for its happy-go-lucky attitude to life. It is a natural clown and loves to play, but can be willful and even naughty at times. However, its adorable flat face and big, expressive eyes mean that it's hard to be cross with a Pug. It is said that once you own a Pug, you will be forever in its thrall.

THE LHASA APSO

This ancient breed takes its name from the sacred city of Lhasa in Tibet, high in the Himalayas. It was owned only by nobility and holy men in its native country, who believed that when its master died, his soul entered the Lhasa Apso's body. It is known in its homeland as *abso seng kye*, which translates as "bark lion sentinel dog."

FACT FILE

COLOR: honey, black, white, slate, parti-color

SIZE (MALE ADULT):
15 pounds (7 kilograms)

HEIGHT AT SHOULDER:
11 inches (28 centimeters)

LIFESPAN: about 15 years

CHARACTER: playful, alert, wary

A SACRED GIFT

The Lhasa Apso was considered lucky in its native country and, because of this high status, it was not allowed to leave Tibet unless given away as a gift by the ruler, the Dalai Lama. The 13th Dalai Lama gave two Lhasa Apsos to American naturalist C. Suydam Cutting in 1930, and he began to breed them.

HARDY LITTLE DOG

The Lhasa Apso—despite its size—is more than capable of surviving in the mountains, where conditions can be harsh. It has a dense double coat that flows over its whole body, falling straight down from the spine on either side to the floor. The hair is silky and needs brushing every day.

WARY AND SUSPICIOUS

Lhasa Apsos are social dogs and make good pets, but they can be willful and difficult to train, and are not good with small children. They can be wary and suspicious—a trait that was valuable in a guard dog—but are also affectionate with the people whom they know and love.

Puppy
—Love—

Whatever the breed you choose, there are few things more lovable than a puppy. With its oversize feet and adoring eyes, it is the most appealing little creature. But the way a puppy starts its life will have an effect on how it behaves for the rest of it, so it is important to make sure everything is done properly.

ACTING ON INSTINCT

For the first three weeks of its life, a puppy is totally dependent on its mother. All it needs is food, sleep, and warmth. Puppies are born deaf and blind, but they do have sense of touch. It is instinct that makes them snuggle up against their mother and suckle from her.

FIRST MILK

As soon as they are born, the puppies will start to suckle, and the first milk that their mother gives them is vital. It is called "colostrum" and is rich with nutrients that will help the puppies to grow strong and healthy. The physical closeness of feeding helps mother and puppies form a bond.

STAYING HEALTHY

Feeding hungry puppies is hard work, and the mother must be fed well while her little ones are relying on her milk. A new mother sometimes loses her appetite after the babies are born, but this does not last for long. She will be feeding her puppies for six weeks, so she needs to keep up her strength.

GROWING STRONGER

The puppies will gain weight rapidly, increasing in size and strength every day. By the fifth day, the puppies should be able to support their weight with their front legs, which makes it easier for them to feed. Their eyes will open after about a week and a half.

A NEW WORLD

By the fourth week, the puppies' teeth will have come through and they can start to eat solid food. They will begin to socialize, and their mother will teach them how to behave and interact with each other. They will start to explore, and to learn their place in the pack. To a pet dog, the pack includes people, too.

READY TO GO

By the seventh week of their life, the puppies will have stopped suckling. They now have sharp little teeth and their mother will push them away! Each puppy has its own independent personality and is ready to be taken to its new home for a loving and happy life.

Farming
Dogs

It is easy to forget how intelligent dogs are and, perhaps more importantly, how much they want to please us. We have used dogs in farming because of their natural instincts to herd and protect sheep, goats, cattle, and other livestock.

THE BORDER COLLIE

The Border Collie was named for the hilly regions on the borders of Wales, Scotland, and England, where it was bred to work. The breed is as good-looking as it is clever. Its herding abilities were soon recognized beyond its homelands, and it became a popular animal worldwide.

RECORD-BREAKING DOG

In May 2016, a 16-month-old Border Collie named Cap smashed the previous world record for a Border Collie when he was sold for £14,805 ($21,262) following a display at a trials competition in North Yorkshire. The previous highest price was £9,240 ($13,270), paid in 2013.

TINY SIGNALS

A silent worker, the Border Collie will respond to its master's tiniest signal, whether a spoken word or a mere twitch of a finger. It will gather its flock in seconds and deftly herd them wherever the shepherd wants them to go. A working Border Collie can run for 50 miles (80 kilometers) or more in a single day.

ENERGY AND DRIVE

With the right training, the Border Collie can make a wonderful family dog. However, because of its energy and drive, it will need a lot of exercise. Its herding instincts mean it will try to round up a flock, which could well be the family of its owner! Border Collies are also born to compete in dog agility competitions.

FACT FILE

COLOR: black and white, brown and white, tricolor, merle

SIZE (MALE ADULT): 45 pounds (20 kilograms)

HEIGHT AT SHOULDER: 22 inches (56 centimeters)

LIFESPAN: about 12 years

CHARACTER: intelligent, loyal, lively

THE KOMONDOR

It may look like a walking mop, but the Komondor has been bred for more than 1,000 years to herd and protect sheep in Hungary. It is descended from dogs that were brought to Hungary by the Cuman people, who lived in ancient China. The name "Komondor" comes from *Cuman-dor*, meaning "dog of the Cumans."

CORDED COAT

The most noticeable feature of the modern Komondor is its extraordinary coat. The outer hair fuses with the undercoat to make thick, felted cords that grow up to 11 inches (28 centimeters) long. The cords take up to two years to grow and help the dog to blend in with the herd of sheep. They also protect it from weather and from any predators, such as wolves, that attack its flock.

RARE BREED

As with many dog breeds, the Komondor almost became extinct after World War II. Thankfully, dedicated breeders managed to save it, though it remains a rare breed. The Komondor is still used as a livestock guardian in rural Hungary—just like its ancestors, centuries before.

UNNERVING STARE

The Komondor has been bred to be fiercely protective, which makes it a challenging pet. It will glare through its bangs at its "flock"—which could well include you—and will continue to watch you as you go about your daily business. It can be suspicious of other dogs, too. But with the right training, it can be a loving family pet.

FACT FILE

COLOR: white

SIZE (MALE ADULT):
100 pounds (45 kilograms)

HEIGHT AT SHOULDER:
27 inches (69 centimeters)

LIFESPAN: about 12 years

CHARACTER: protective, confident, active

THE SAMOYED

The "Sammy smile" is irresistible! The Samoyed's mouth turns slightly upward at the corners, making it look like the dog is smiling. It is indeed a happy dog, and loves people. This trait probably comes from its history of closeness with the Samoyed people, who originally bred the dog to herd reindeer in Siberia.

HARSH CONDITIONS

The Samoyeds lived and worked on the Taymyr Peninsula, the most northern point of Siberia, known for its cold, harsh conditions. As well as herding, the dogs pulled sleds, hunted game, and protected their people from predators. They shared their living space and helped to keep them warm.

TWO COATS

To keep out the cold, a Samoyed has a very thick, dense coat, which consists of a woolly undercoat and longer outer coat. The dog can easily shake snow off of its tough, protective outer coat. But in the spring, the Samoyed will shed ... and shed ... and shed! The Samoyed people would spin this hair and weave it like sheep's wool to make warm clothing.

ATTENTION LOVER

It is said that a bad-tempered Samoyed doesn't exist! The breed is good-natured and playful, and always happy to be with people. It is active, curious, mischievous, and just wants attention. It makes a perfect family dog, because it loves children, but it can be destructive if it gets bored.

FACT FILE

COLOR: white, cream, biscuit

SIZE (MALE ADULT):
60 pounds (27 kilograms)

HEIGHT AT SHOULDER:
24 inches (61 centimeters)

LIFESPAN: about 14 years

CHARACTER: loving, happy, intelligent

THE OLD ENGLISH SHEEPDOG

The extravagant coat of the Old English Sheepdog suggests that there is some Poodle in its heritage, though its exact origins are unknown. It was bred in the western counties of England by farmers who needed an intelligent and fast-moving dog to drive their livestock to market.

WEALTHY OWNERS

The first American to own an Old English Sheepdog was a Mr W. Wade from Pittsburgh in the late 1880s. By the turn of the century, the breed was still very rare in the United States, and only five wealthy U.S. families owned the breed. The judges at the 1904 Westminster Show in New York were advised to "take plenty of time; the dogs in the ring are the property of some of our leading Americans."

BOBTAIL DOGS

When farmers sheared their sheep in the spring, they would shear the dogs' coats, too, and use the hair to make warm clothing. In 18th century England, there was a tax on working dogs with tails, so farmers would often dock their dogs' tails to avoid having to pay the tax. Because of this, Old English Sheepdogs were sometimes called Bobtails. Many people now think that docking is cruel, and it is banned in some countries.

LOTS OF EXERCISE

Although it is a big, boisterous dog bred for work, the Old English Sheepdog makes an adorable family pet. It does require lots of exercise, and that gorgeous coat needs a lot of care, but it is loving and lovable, and protective of its family and friends. Its deep bark will frighten off any intruder!

FACT FILE

COLOR: gray, grizzle, blue or blue merle, brown, and fawn, with white markings

SIZE (MALE ADULT): 65 pounds (29 kilograms)

HEIGHT AT SHOULDER: 24 inches (61 centimeters)

LIFESPAN: about 12 years

CHARACTER: friendly, loyal, gentle

THE WELSH CORGI

There are two recognized types of Corgi: the Pembroke and the Cardigan. The Cardigan is thought to be the older of the two, with a history reaching back to the 13th century. It was also known as the "yard dog," because it measures one yard (3 feet or 90 centimeters) from the tip of its nose to the end of its outstretched tail.

IMPRESSIVE TAIL

The Cardigan Corgi is larger than its cousin, and its coat comes in a greater variety of colors. For a small breed, it has an impressive tail—long, heavy, and hanging low, almost reaching the ground. It sometimes has a marking on its back that is known as a "fairy saddle," from a legend that once upon a time, fairies rode the little dogs.

A QUEEN'S FAVORITE

The Pembroke Corgi is more famous, because it is the favorite dog breed of Queen Elizabeth II of the United Kingdom. She has owned more than 30 Corgis during her reign. It is easy to see why—the little dog has a charmingly foxy face and a happy nature.

FACT FILE

COLOR: red, sable, brindle, black, blue merle, white markings

SIZE (MALE ADULT): 38 pounds (17 kilograms)

HEIGHT AT SHOULDER: 12 inches (30 centimeters)

LIFESPAN: about 15 years

CHARACTER: alert, clever, stubborn

AFFECTIONATE PETS

Although they were once used to herd cattle, Welsh Corgis are now bred as pets. They make delightful companions, since they are affectionate with adults as well as with children. The Cardigan tends to be more reserved than the Pembroke.

Pets

WITH A PURPOSE

Dogs have been by our side for so long and today, perhaps more than ever, they are thought of as companions, rather than co-workers. But the jobs we expect our dogs to do have shaped their behavior and abilities, and most have retained those traits. Some are still in use today.

THE SIBERIAN HUSKY

One of the most beautiful dog breeds, the Siberian Husky—sometimes called the Arctic Husky—looks in many ways like its ancestor, the gray wolf. The breed comes in many colors, with striking patterns on its gorgeous face. The Husky is also known for its startling ice-blue eyes.

LIFE-SAVING SLED DOGS

In eastern Siberia, the Husky was used by the Chukchi people as a long-distance sled dog. In 1909, several Huskies were brought to Alaska to compete in races. In 1925, Husky dog teams brought life-saving medicine to the isolated town of Nome, Alaska, where a diphtheria epidemic had broken out.

SNOWSHOE FEET

The Husky is able to cope with really cold weather: its thick double coat can protect it in temperatures as low as -76 degrees Fahrenheit (-60 degrees Celsius). Its large feet have tufts of fur between the toes and act like snowshoes, keeping the feet warm and providing grip on the ice.

EAGER TO PLEASE

The Husky instinctively knows that it was bred to haul a sled. When you put a leash on one, it will try to pull your arms out! However, it makes a lovely pet, with a sweet, happy nature and eager-to-please attitude. The Chukchi held their dogs in high esteem, and kept them in the family home. In addition, because they had to work as a team, these dogs learned to be friendly and amenable.

FACT FILE

COLOR: all colors

SIZE (MALE ADULT):
60 pounds (27 kilograms)

HEIGHT AT SHOULDER:
24 inches (61 centimeters)

LIFESPAN: about 15 years

CHARACTER: docile, friendly, energetic

THE DALMATIAN

Spotted dogs have a long history as well as an enduring appeal. They have existed in Africa, Europe, and Asia for centuries and have even appeared in Egyptian sculpture. The Dalmatian takes its name from Dalmatia, a coastal region in what is now Croatia. However, the exact origins of the breed are unclear.

PROTECTION FROM ROBBERS

A handsome animal, the Dalmatian was used in Europe in the Middle Ages as a hunting dog. Later, it became a common sight in England, running alongside or even underneath carriages. Its flashy appearance added to the vehicle's elegance and protected its passengers from robbers on horseback.

FIREHOUSE DOG

In the United States, the Dalmatian also became known as the "firehouse dog," because it would run in front of horse-drawn fire engines and guard them when they were not in use. It was a companion for the horses, too. Many fire stations still keep the tradition alive by having a Dalmatian as their mascot.

FACT FILE

COLOR: white with black or liver (brown) spots

SIZE (MALE ADULT):
55 pounds (25 kilograms)

HEIGHT AT SHOULDER:
24 inches (60 centimeters)

LIFESPAN: about 12 years

CHARACTER: friendly, protective, loving

WITHOUT SPOTS

Dalmatians are now kept mostly as pets. They make loving and protective companions, but they do need a lot of attention. They are active dogs and must have plenty of exercise. Although they are best known for their striking spots, Dalmatian puppies are born pure white, and their spots appear as they grow older.

THE SCHNAUZER

The Schnauzer, a German breed, comes in three sizes: miniature, giant, and standard. The Standard Schnauzer is thought to be the oldest of the three, so it forms the basis of the breed. The Schnauzer was bred to be an all-purpose working dog on German farms—ratting, herding livestock, and guarding the family.

ARISTOCRATIC APPEARANCE

The Schnauzer is a handsome, intelligent dog, with a stiff, wiry coat that isn't prone to much shedding, and has little "doggy" smell. It has impressive arched eyebrows and a bristling mustache and beard, which give it an aristocratic appearance. The dog carries itself with bustling self-importance!

MULTIPURPOSE

That sense of self-worth is not misplaced. The Schnauzer is agile and athletic and capable of many jobs. It has been used as a hunting dog and will happily retrieve game on land or in water. It was much in demand as a drover before railroads ended the need for dogs to help drive livestock to market. It also makes an excellent watchdog.

FACT FILE

COLOR: all shades of pepper-and-salt gray, pure black

SIZE (STANDARD): 50 pounds (23 kilograms)

HEIGHT AT SHOULDER: 20 inches (51 centimeters)

LIFESPAN: about 16 years

CHARACTER: dignified, curious, devoted

EAGER TO PLEASE

Like many clever dogs, the Schnauzer can be stubborn. But it does have a will to please and, if trained properly, makes a rewarding pet. It gets bored easily and loves to learn new tricks, so it does very well in agility classes. It has lots of energy and requires plenty of exercise.

THE DOBERMAN PINSCHER

Tax collectors were rarely popular people, but one named Louis Dobermann is credited with developing this handsome and imposing breed. He was also the town dogcatcher and often took a dog with him on his rounds for protection from bandits.

GERMAN BLOODLINES

Dobermann began trying to breed a dog that would be a loyal companion as well as a fierce protector. Although he never revealed the exact bloodlines he used, it is thought that they included the Rottweiler, German Pinscher, and Black-and-Tan Terrier.

ONLY THE BEST

Those early Doberman Pinschers were bred to be intimidating and aggressive, which unfortunately has not helped the breed's reputation. When the first "Dobies" were shown in the United States in the 1900s, it is said that they won "best in show" honors at three shows without even having their teeth looked at—the judges were too scared to inspect them!

FACT FILE

COLOR: black, red, blue, isabella (fawn)

SIZE (MALE ADULT): 88 pounds (40 kilograms)

HEIGHT AT SHOULDER: 28 inches (71 centimeters)

LIFESPAN: about 13 years

CHARACTER: loyal, alert, fearless

FUN-LOVING AND PLAYFUL

Today's Doberman Pinscher is a calmer and more gentle dog. It is still a natural protector, but is fun-loving and playful with children. It has also been a success as a therapy dog in nursing homes, a far cry from its original purpose. However, as a large animal, it does need plenty of exercise.

THE GREAT DANE

The "great" in its name doesn't merely apply to its size: dog lovers will tell you that everything about this breed is great! It is sometimes known as the "Apollo of dogs." Apollo is the Greek god of the Sun, which gives you an idea of just how highly prized this breed is.

ANCIENT BREED

The Great Dane has been around for a long time. Drawings on Egyptian monuments dating back to 3000 B.C. resemble the breed, and dogs that sound like Great Danes are also mentioned in Chinese literature from around 1121 B.C. Massive Mastiff-like dogs were brought to parts of Europe in 407 A.D. They were used to hunt bears and wild boar, and they became known as boarhounds. These dogs were the ancestors of today's Great Danes.

DANISH DOG

It wasn't until the 18th century that the dog got its present name. A French naturalist saw a version of the boarhound in Denmark that was more refined and more like a Greyhound than a Mastiff type. He called this dog *Grand Danois*, which soon became the "Great Danish Dog," even though the breed did not originate in Denmark.

LOVING AND GENTLE

Despite its size, the Great Dane really is a gentle giant. Once it was no longer used to hunt boar, its fierce nature was bred out. It is loving and gentle, even if it sometimes doesn't realize quite how big it is and thinks it's fine to drape itself across your lap. It also has a tendency to head-butt you for attention!

FACT FILE

COLOR: fawn, brindle, blue, black, harlequin, mantle

SIZE (MALE ADULT): 200 pounds (90 kilograms)

HEIGHT AT SHOULDER: 34 inches (86 centimeters)

LIFESPAN: about 10 years

CHARACTER: gentle, affectionate, protective

THE NEWFOUNDLAND

The "Newfie," as it's affectionately known, comes from the same part of Canada as the Labrador Retriever, which was once known as the lesser Newfoundland dog. Whether the two breeds are related is open to debate, but they are similar in many ways. They were both bred to help fishermen.

VIKING BEAR DOG

Another theory about their origin is that the Newfoundland is a descendant of the Vikings' black "bear dogs," brought to the continent around 1000 A.D. Skeletons of large dogs were discovered at a Viking settlement on the northern tip of Newfoundland in the 1950s. They may also be related to the Tibetan Mastiff.

FAMOUS FAN

By the late 18th century, the Newfoundland had almost died out, but in the 19th century the English artist Edwin Landseer helped to make the breed popular again. Some of his paintings featured Newfoundlands in heroic roles. The black-and-white version of the breed is named the Landseer in his honor.

A BIG SOFTIE

It is no coincidence that Nana, the gentle, lovable dog that featured in J. M. Barrie's classic children's story *Peter Pan*, was a Newfoundland. It may be huge, but this Canadian dog is a big softie that loves all people, especially children. It was originally bred as a working dog, but makes a wonderful pet.

FACT FILE

COLOR: mostly black,
Landseer (white and black),
brown, gray

SIZE (MALE ADULT):
120 pounds (54 kilograms)

HEIGHT AT SHOULDER:
29 inches (74 centimeters)

LIFESPAN: about 15 years

CHARACTER: patient,
intelligent, loving

THE ROTTWEILER

Long ago in Germany, a breed of imposing black-and-tan Mastiff-type dogs became known for their skill at helping drive livestock to market. They were named after the town of Rottweil, a center of livestock trading. They may have been brought to Germany by Roman soldiers.

GUARD DOGS

The Romans used these dogs to guard their livestock, but let them go once the livestock had been eaten. Like their ancestors, Rottweilers were big and imposing, with a natural instinct to guard and protect. They herded cattle and pulled carts of meat to the market. After selling their livestock, the cattlemen kept their money safe from thieves by putting their purses around their dog's neck when they journeyed home.

GUARD AND PROTECT

The modern Rottweiler has retained its natural guarding instincts and, although it did have a reputation for being fierce, it is not aggressive by nature. But it is brave and will hold its ground, so it is still popular as a guard dog today. Its proud looks are usually enough of a deterrent!

FACT FILE

COLOR: black and tan

SIZE: 130 pounds
(59 kilograms)

HEIGHT AT SHOULDER:
27 inches (69 centimeters)

LIFE SPAN: about 11 years

CHARACTER: intelligent,
gentle, confident

CALM AND GENTLE

Their protective instincts have served the Rottweiler well. Despite its ferocious appearance, it is a gentle and calm dog that will defend its family to its last breath if necessary. It is intelligent but needs firm training to make it into a loving member of the family.

Unusual
Breeds

The range of dog breeds across the world is immense, and some look like they weren't planned very carefully! But as with all natural breeds, there is a reason for the more unusual appearance of some dogs and, underneath, they are all still "man's best friend."

THE XOLOITZCUINTLI

The name of this breed—pronounced *show-low-etz-queent-lee*—comes from the name of the Aztec god Xolotl and the Aztec word for dog, *itzcuintli*. But it is no wonder that this extraordinary breed is generally known as the Xolo, or more often as the Mexican hairless.

FIRST DOG

The Xolo is certainly one of the world's oldest and rarest breeds. Archaeological evidence shows that thousands of years ago, the Xolo's earliest ancestors probably migrated with early humans across a land bridge that existed between Asia and North America. The Xolo can therefore justly be called the "first dog of the Americas."

HEALING POWERS?

Perhaps because of its unusual appearance, the Xoloitzcuintli was believed to have healing powers. In remote Mexican and Central American villages, it was kept to ward off evil spirits, as well as ailments such as painful joints, asthma, toothache, and trouble sleeping.

WARM SKIN

Although there is a variety that does have hair, most Xolos are hairless. This lack of fur means they don't look very cuddly. However, a Xolo's skin is very warm, and the breed makes a loving and faithful companion. It is sometimes called the "velcro dog" because it sticks with its owner! As an intelligent breed, it needs attention and stimulation, but is easily trained.

FACT FILE

COLOR: black, slate, gray,
bronze, brindle, red, fawn
(solid or spotted)

SIZE (MALE ADULT):
50 pounds (23 kilograms)

HEIGHT AT SHOULDER:
24 inches (61 centimeters)

LIFESPAN: about 20 years

CHARACTER: affectionate,
intelligent, curious

THE AFGHAN HOUND

There are few dogs more glamorous than the Afghan Hound. With its slender, elegant face and flowing silky fur, it is the supermodel of the dog world. It comes from Afghanistan, where it was known as the *Tazi*, and is one of the world's oldest breeds, dating back thousands of years.

HUNTING LEOPARDS

The Afghan is a sight hound, meaning that it hunts by sight rather than by scent. It was used to hunt wild goats, wolves, and snow leopards in the mountains of its home country. Its beautiful coat was not just for show; the long hair protected it from the cold of the mountains as well as the heat of the desert.

SHOWBIZ FAVORITE

The breed was brought to England in the 1900s, with the first being exhibited in the country in 1907. Zeppo Marx of the famed comedy act, the Marx Brothers, was among the first to bring the dogs to the United States. The famous doll Barbie was sold with a pet Afghan Hound called Beauty, making the breed popular with little girls.

SWEET-NATURED

Bred to be an independent hunter, the Afghan Hound can be rather aloof, and will only want affection on its own terms. But it is sweet-natured and rarely aggressive. It needs a lot of exercise and, as a sight hound, is likely to take off and chase something if it is not kept on a leash.

FACT FILE

COLOR: black, blue, red, cream, gold, silver, brindle, oyster

SIZE (MALE ADULT):
64 pounds (29 kilograms)

HEIGHT AT SHOULDER:
28 inches (74 centimeters)

LIFESPAN: about 14 years

CHARACTER: independent, aloof, sweet

THE TIBETAN MASTIFF

Mastiff-type dogs originated in the foothills of the Himalayas, on the edge of Tibet, around 5,000 years ago. They developed into two kinds: the *Do-Kyhi*, which were used to guard flocks of sheep, and the bigger *Tsang-Khyi*, which served as guardians for the Tibetan Buddhist monks.

ANCIENT BREED

Although it is known to be an ancient breed, there is little information about the Tibetan Mastiff before 1800, when a Captain Samuel Turner mentioned "huge dogs" in his memoir of his time in Tibet. He did not describe the dogs in any detail, but it is likely that they were Tibetan Mastiffs.

MILLION–DOLLAR DOGS

With its massive head, muscular body, strong legs, and thick, shaggy fur, the Tibetan Mastiff is a handsome animal. They are so desirable that a golden Tibetan Mastiff puppy was sold for $2 million in 2014. Since then prices have dropped somewhat, but they are by no means a cheap pet!

FACT FILE

COLOR: black, black and tan, gold, gray

SIZE (MALE ADULT):
170 pounds (77 kilograms)

HEIGHT AT SHOULDER:
28 inches (71 centimeters)

LIFESPAN: about 12 years

CHARACTER: strong-willed, calm, protective

STRONG-WILLED

Despite its bear-like appearance, the Tibetan Mastiff is a gentle and quiet dog. A born guardian, it is extremely protective, and has its own ideas about who is a friend and who is an enemy! It can be strong-willed and stubborn, and is not a breed suited to a first-time dog owner.

THE SHAR-PEI

The name "Shar-Pei" means "sand-skin." Statues that look much like the modern Shar-Pei have been found in the southern provinces of China, dating back to around 200 B.C. More recently, a Chinese manuscript from the 13th century refers to dogs with wrinkled skin.

FOLDS AND WRINKLES

The Shar-Pei looks like it is wearing the skin of a much bigger animal! But those folds and wrinkles, and the rough, sandy texture of its coat, serve a purpose. The breed was developed as a hunting dog and a guardian. Those loose rolls meant that any animal that tried to fight a Shar-Pei merely got a mouthful of bristly skin.

SAVE THE SHAR-PEI!

Unfortunately, this unusual breed was almost lost. China's Communist rulers disapproved of owning dogs as pets, and many thousands of dogs were killed. In 1973, a Hong Kong breeder named Matgo Law appealed to American dog breeders to "save the Chinese Shar-Pei." The Chinese Shar-Pei Club of America was formed the very next year.

FACT FILE

COLOR: all colors

SIZE (MALE ADULT):
55 pounds (25 kilograms)

HEIGHT AT SHOULDER:
20 inches (51 centimeters)

LIFESPAN: about 12 years

CHARACTER: independent, calm, loyal

STUBBORN STREAK

This is a dog that just loves people! The Shar-Pei is said to prefer people to other dogs and likes to be with its owner as much as possible. It is devoted to and protective of its human family, but it does have a stubborn streak and can be strong-willed. It needs kind but firm leadership from its earliest days.

THE CHOW CHOW

In China, it was known as *Songshi Quan*, which means "puffy lion dog," and looking at the Chow Chow, you can see why. With its stocky stance and fluffy coat, it is an impressive creature. It is thought to be one of the oldest of all breeds, perhaps the first domestic dog that evolved from the wolf.

A DOG OF MANY NAMES

The Chow Chow was also called *hei shi-tou* ("black-tongue dog") because it is one of only two breeds to have a blue-black tongue. Other names include *lang gou* ("wolf dog") and *xiang gou* ("bear dog"). British merchants carried these bear-like dogs in their cargo. Miscellaneous items of cargo were traditionally called "Chow Chow," and the name stuck.

EXTREMELY STRONG

The Chow Chow is extremely strong, but has a rather stilted, short-striding gait. In its native country, the Chow Chow was prized as a guard dog and a hunter. One Chinese emperor was said to have kept 2,500 Chow Chows for hunting. The dogs were also used to pull sleds, herd livestock, and protect boats as well as the home.

A CANINE TEDDY BEAR

It might be hard to see its expression under all that fur, but the Chow Chow has a generally sweet nature, although it can be aloof. An intelligent dog, the Chow Chow will dominate if it is allowed to. But it is said that the breed combines the nobility of a lion, the comedy of a panda, the appeal of a teddy bear, and the grace of a cat.

FACT FILE

COLOR: red, black, blue, fawn, cinnamon, cream, gray, white

SIZE (MALE ADULT): 70 pounds (32 kilograms)

HEIGHT AT SHOULDER: 22 inches (56 centimeters)

LIFESPAN: about 15 years

CHARACTER: intelligent, loyal, aloof

INDEX